WHO
WILL KNOW US?

New Poems

by

G A R Y   S O T O

D0188379

CHRONICLE BOOKS

San Francisco

Printed in the United States of America.

Library of Congress Cataloging in Publication Data

Soto, Gary.
    Who will know us? : poems / by Gary Soto.
       p.   cm.
    ISBN (invalid) 0-87701-740-4. — ISBN 0-87701-673-9 (pbk.)
    I. Title.
    PS3569.072W54   1990   89-22047
    811'.54–dc20   CIP

Distributed in Canada by Raincoast Books, 112 East Third Avenue,
Vancouver, B.C. V5T IC8

10 9 8 7 6 5 4 3 2 1

CHRONICLE BOOKS
275 Fifth Street
San Francisco, California 94103

Acknowledgements

Many of these poems first appeared in the following magazines: THE BLOOMSBURY REVIEW, CRAZY HORSE, 5 AM, THE MISSOURI REVIEW, MSS, THE NATION, THE NEW REPUBLIC, THE OHIO REVIEW, ONTARIO REVIEW, PLOUGHSHARES, STAND, THE THREEPENNY REVIEW, and ZYZZYVA.

"Sorrow in French," "That Girl," "Small Town with One Road," "Heaven," "The Seventieth Year," "Rough Translation of a Sabine's Poem," "Ars Poetica, or Mazatlan, on a Day When Bodies Wash to the Shore," "Elegy," "Who Will Know Us?" and "Worry at the End of the Month" first appeared in POETRY.

This book is for Chris, Ernesto, and Jon—amigos.

CONTENTS

THREE 🐚

ONE ❧

You're in this dream of cotton plants.
You raise a hoe, swing, and the first weeds
Fall with a sigh. You take another step,
Chop, and the sigh comes again,
Until you yourself are breathing that way
With each step, a sigh that will follow you into town.

That's hours later. The sun is a red blister
Coming up in your palm. Your back is strong,
Young, not yet the broken chair
In an abandoned school of dry spiders.
Dust settles on your forehead, dirt
Smiles under each fingernail.
You chop, step, and by the end of the first row,
You can buy one splendid fish for wife
And three sons. Another row, another fish,
Until you have enough and move on to milk,
Bread, meat. Ten hours and the cupboards creak.
You can rest in the back yard under a tree.
Your hands twitch on your lap,
Not unlike the fish on a pier or the bottom
Of a boat. You drink iced tea. The minutes jerk
Like flies.
                    It's dusk, now night,
And the lights in your home are on.
That costs money, yellow light
In the kitchen. That's thirty steps,
You say to your hands,
Now shaped into binoculars.
You could raise them to your eyes:
You were a fool in school, now look at you.
You're a giant among cotton plants,
The lung-shaped leaves that run breathing for miles.

Now you see your oldest boy, also running.
Papa, he says, it's time to come in,
You pull him into your lap
And ask, What's forty times nine?
He knows as well as you, and you smile.
The wind makes peace with the trees,
The stars strike themselves in the dark.
You get up and walk with the sigh of cotton plants.
You go to sleep with a red sun on your palm,
The sore light you see when you first stir in bed. ❧

The stars are eating through the sky
Now that it's twilight, hour
When in the backyard
I can do no more than a tree:
Bend, flutter, root myself in wind.
For me guilt keeps the flesh going.
I look around. The pond is blowing
With lines. The fuchsia, bright lantern
Of flowers, moves in the breeze,
And our cat scratches on the fence.
And what I don't see I hear:
Daughter in her room cutting paper
With toy scissors. My wife
Is in the front yard, watering.
This all stops. I give myself over
To what uncle said: that it was father,
Then dead three years, and his steps
Rounding the house to the back porch
Twice a week — crunch of gravel
And a presence at the door.
When I close my eyes, he's on the steps,
Brow of sadness, his Pendleton open
From the wind that climbs the junkyard —
Along the alley, silhouette of iron
And pipes held against the sky.
That's how we leave. We die in
Such places. Like father,
Whom we miss and don't know,
Who would have saved us
From those terrible years
If that day at work he got up
Hurt but alive. He fell
From that ladder with an upturned palm,
With the eyes of watery light.

We went on with sorrow that found no tree
To cry from. I can't go to his grave.
I know this. I can't find my place
Or wake up and say, Let him walk,
Let him round the house but not come in.
Even the sun with so much to give must fall. ❧

We hear you want to die.
What is it?
The hair on an arm
Leaning toward the shadows?

Sun-Maid is gone, Grandpa,
The machinery fleeced in rust.
Though the loading dock holds the years
Of rain, sweat that fell
And opened into momentary coins.
Work has stopped. You can sleep now.
Sunlight enters the house,
Dust drifts in a galaxy
Of unmapped motes. And Grandma?
She is well—her veins no longer
Surfacing under a blue flesh.
She's with you now
And you smell the warmth
Of her nightly presence.
Get up and eat, Grandpa.
Your skin has yellowed.
Look at the back yard garden—
Already the flower beds
Brim with summer weeds
And ants unravel
From their dark holes in the trees.
Come to the kitchen.
It is warm there, Grandpa,
And your family, the little ones
With their cards of Get Well,
Has gathered like a small cloud,
Like the steam weeping
On the window. ૨૭

Something must happen. Someone must
Rule who can cry and believe
In the permanent. I worry
About the earth and the absence of Father,
And how we tear our hands
For what's not ours. The eagle
Gives up its bones. On their hooks
Pigs kick blood in the faces of workers.

And even the sea, flat green
From where I look, is giving up
At the shore—gray whale
That's cut with initials, or worse.
Children did this. And men.
I face this daily. The newspaper
Runs its one story, Thursday or Friday.

We love to kill with what
We've made from rocks. And so
It would take a God drifting across water
To save what's left. Or a redemptive
Tree to leap from, one by one,
Until the world is so quiet
We won't know this place
Or remember to get up
And begin where we left off. ❧

They say that it's not at all white,
That the freeze going up
Is momentary,

Then the full remembrance:
The alley with its morning fog,
Father, piping soup
On the stove's blue rings.
Then the *and* and *and* of a child's first years.

Maybe you sit in a chair.
Maybe earth is far below.
The string that ties you to that place
Is just a waver,
Spider skein two thousand years down.

Or maybe the new home is much closer,
Just above the trees,
A sea howl at the window
—or you're those hangers banging
Quietly when the closet door opens.

Conjectures. Little clues,
Really. But we're hopeful that we'll wake.
The chair is for us. The sorting
Of days is done on our fingers.

Lost boot, first girl,
Scar on the chin with its pink hook. ❧

HOUSE, STREET, OLD MAN

Toy tractor under the house, empty clock,
Plumbing that howls like the sea
Within the walls,

And the walls dirty-white where the cat rubbed
And the child of splashed milk
Giggled over a finger game.

Sister roaring places. Wet truck.
Sky making room for clouds, that black threat
Over the grocery, something

For Mr. Bandini to think about
On his porch. Not much
Time for that.

Tomorrow he rolls his car.
His arms freeze
Going up

To that place. The usual white
Squaring off in the eyes. &

E L E G Y

for Sadao Oda

The mountain, snow-covered in April,
And the bushes at our feet, along the cliffs,
Firing into tiger-orange blossoms.
Early morning and we drive toward Sequoia,
To get away from the house, the dead hours
And sadness, black branch of sparrows, just out the window.
We went by Belmont, past Minkler and Old Town,
And tried to be happy not once but twice—
Bought apples from a farmer with root-cold hands,
Watched sheep, fat as couches, on a green roll of hill.
When we called, they turned the other way.
When we slammed the car door, they looked back,
Their eyes of wet stone.

At a toppled roadside stand, five thousand
Feet above the valley, the haze
Is feather-colored, far away
Like you who are no longer with us,
You who in your time thinned grapes,
Hoed beets, stood muddy in boots,
The waters of twilight filling the rows of cotton.
Work. Work and fish is what you did.
Saintly in the shine of your work-polished clothes
You skinned the persimmon with an ancient knife,
Assuring your granddaughter, "This is good. You'll see."
In this air, thin-blue, we don't say much.
Wind plays in our hair. A bee circles lazily
The sweetness of a crushed can.
Not yet noon, and already we're losing the day. ❧

The earth already knows too much
About us. We dig holes
And throw ourselves in,
Weep, set stones
Where no stone would sleep.

The mountains, blue yoke in the distance,
Are coming down—
Rock, bush, slaughtered tree.

The sea is washing salt from the bodies
Over and over, and without rest.

I tell my daughter, It's not so bad.
She holds up a bombed city
In a book. When she looks
Away, I look away.
                    I put down
My newspaper, gray gauze of words,
And want to beat this country with a stick
Or pipe, wake it from this madness
That eats anything that doesn't speak.

But what can I do with these hands?
Push people back, stop a car,
Wave for help on the front lawn?

Shame is picked away from under a thumbnail.
God circles above. The street
Is like any other, and east or west,
Our end is only a stone
That won't roll back. 🙢

MOSES

for Jon's collie

Someone is thinking of you, Moses,
Right now, and it's Tuesday,
Not Sunday when some robed God
Is fooling in the trees.
Do you remember our friends?
We sat in backyards. The wine
Was uncorked, the glasses blood-red
At dusk and the steaks hissing
On the grill—laughter
Under the arbor, laughter
For the grape, the plum
That was water in our hands.
A cracker for you on those evenings,
Wedge of cheese, chicken fat,
Buttered bread flung into the air.
We drank, ate, pitched bocce balls
Into the crooked garden.
Drunk, we couldn't think right.
You did. You rolled onto your side
And sighed for the love of abundant grass.
We could have learned the street's harvest
From you and how to race for
The female without breathing hard.
As it was, we scratched your ears.
We whined our nickel-and-dime fortunes
And slouched before the coals,
Talking poorly about death.
But you were the strong one.
A month later you bit a mouthful
Of earth and trotted into a blind car—
A lesson for us living in chairs.
Now it's Tuesday. The trees
Are trying to amuse me before dinner.

I look back. You were the one.
You died gallantly, as a friend said,
With your feet straight in the air.
The blood, the loud engines,
The world stopped in your very bones. &

E V E

It was on your father's workbench
In the barn that you undid
Your skirt: hair, kinked hair
Thick as a child's black scribbling,
Pink when you breathed
And opened. You watched
Me watch you. The barn ticked.
Pigeons shifted in the rafters,
Their wings like prayers as we made
Hurt noises and blood cried from
A new wound. Scared, you left,
And I counted to a hundred
Before I walked out. Shame
Rode on my shoes with the dust.
I looked up. Your father,
A good man, was on the ditch bank,
Irrigating. I drank water
From the hose, watched you watch me.
You climbed back up the fruit ladder
With a peach bucket on your hip.

I was a boy. I hurried home, scared
By then, because the bucket
Was a baby nine months
From that morning when we said
"Let's try," and pulled at each other,
The bench chirping from a loose bolt,
Or was it love and that bolt?
How we thought we knew. Big friends
Said it should hurt the first time,
Then stop, that we would become
Man and woman, and drive long cars,
—life like a pinwheel in the air.
Eve, country girl with babies
Like melons, with no daddy
For the crying—how they lied. ❧

The apricot is down, piled in rain–dark barrels.
The shovel leans against the garage,
Along with caked hoe and leaf-stuck rake,

And the new grass is a beard
On the face of old earth. You worked there,
Pulled roots and leveled your space into lines.

The cement walk between zinnias and green beans
Is jagged with the first ants. Rain water
Is in coffee cans, still rippling

From cat's whiskers. Hunger is a missed meal,
Prayer, crossed shadows from the telephone wire,
And your one provision during Lent

Is to sit still. Clouds make it possible.
Cloud and the bee that has thrown a tree into blossom,
The apple is in blossom, the pear and dwarf plum,

And the Iceland poppy along the graveled drive.
The new grass, like us, will have no place to go
But up, through its terrible cuttings. ❧

The whacked fly
Is put to use
By the cat.
The cat rolls
Onto her back,
Is clever. The pond
Ripples, even without fish,
And the hotel lawn
Is sucking the
Straws of moisture.
The bee, once dead
For autumn,
Now throws faint
Shadows on clover.
And me? I'm sitting
Before the house salad,
Pounding idiot drool
Of bleu cheese
From a slow bottle.
I'm having chicken
Wings for dinner
And will, as last night,
Carry these wings
To the Ohio River.
Water has a place
To go when the moon climbs
Down to wash among
The waves. For me
Home is west,
Further than the river
Will reach, or clouds.
I'm dead lonely.
My wings are useless.
The moon dips
Into the water
And comes up as morning. ❧

We drove looking for that place,
Academy Cemetery, and found broken asphalt,
Fence posts, cows with boulder–sized heads
Hanging over barbed wire, drooling.
We looked at one another and turned off the radio.
It seemed that we were lost, and we slowed
The car until its shadow caught up. Brown grass
Glittered bottles and the cellophane
Wrappers of cigarette packs, flattened cans,
Pie tins, and sheet metal. We pulled to the side,
Got out, and walked with hands in our pockets,
Both of us loving the sound
Of gravel under foot. It was Saturday
In Fresno, but in the foothills, a quiet Sunday.
We walked without saying much,
A nod at a bird, a tap on the shoulder
When rabbits sprang across the road.
The cemetery was close by we knew,
Over that ridge, behind the rise of railroad track.
The dead can't get up and just go,
We thought, and stood in the sun,
Cheated by our dollar map.
                    But when the wind picked up,
When a leaf sparkled we guessed the three oak trees.
When we started over, running uphill,
The grass grew tall enough to whisper at our thighs. ❧

WHO WILL KNOW US?

for Jaroslav Seifert

It is cold, bitter as a penny.
I'm on a train, rocking toward the cemetery
To visit the dead who now
Breathe through the grass, through me,
Through relatives who will come
And ask, Where are you?
Cold. The train with its cargo
Of icy coal, the conductor
With his loose buttons like heads of crucified saints,
His mad puncher biting zeros through tickets.

The window that looks onto its slate of old snow.
Cows. The barbed fences throat-deep in white.
Farm houses dark, one wagon
With a shivering horse.
This is my country, white with no words,
House of silence, horse that won't budge
To cast a new shadow. Fence posts
That are the people, spotted cows the machinery
That feed Officials. I have nothing
Good to say. I love Paris
And write, "Long Live Paris!"
I love Athens and write,
"The great book is still in her lap."
Bats have intrigued me,
The pink vein in a lilac.
I've longed to open an umbrella
In an English rain, smoke
And not give myself away,
Drink and call a friend across the room,
Stomp my feet at the smallest joke.
But this is my country.
I walk a lot, sleep.
I eat in my room, read in my room,
And make up women in my head—
Nostalgia, the cigarette lighter from before the war,
Beauty, tears that flow inward to feed its roots.

The train. Red coal of evil.
We are its passengers, the old and young alike.
Who will know us when we breathe through the grass? ❧

Two

I click the plastic faces of kewpie dolls
Together—they want to kiss but can't.
The magnets behind their heads have died
Out, and wouldn't pull up iron filings
From the loosest dirt, let alone show
Affection, smack lips or clunk heads
And make my bashful nephew say,
Ah, that's for sissies.
                            They stare at each other,
Shyly with hands behind their backs,
Black lash of youth, pink cheeks of first time.
But it's over for them. The magnets
Have died out. I drink my coffee
And think of old girlfriends,
How we too clunked heads together,
Kissed and clunked until that pull of love
Stopped and we just looked.

Sometimes the magnets fall from our heads,
Settle in our hips. Beds are ruined
This way. Books tumble from crowded shelves
When couples clunk waists together,
With the women looking at ceilings,
Men at loose hair on pillows,
And then it's the other way around.
But magnets die out. They grow heavy,
These stones that could sharpen knives
Or bring faces together for one last kiss.

For years I thought iron lived forever,
Certainly longer than love. Now I have doubts.
The kewpie dolls, set on starched doilies
On my grandmother's television,
Smile but don't touch. The paint is flaking,
Dust is a faint aura of loss. Grandmother loved
Her husband for five decades, and still does,
Poor grandpa who is gone. They worked

Side by side in fields, boxed raisins,
Raised children in pairs. Now grandmother
Wants to die but doesn't know how.
Her arms are frail, her eyes of cataract
Can't hold a face. *Hijo, hijo,*
She says, and looks over my shoulder.
It's blinding wisdom to see her on the edge
of her couch. The magnet is in her feet,
Ready to gather up the earth. ❧

It was suffering that I couldn't stab
Like a bug and stop. Russia
Was cheating us out of rain,
China out of air.
In bed disease scared me—
People woke up and it was there,
Like a baseball under the skin,
A vest of darker blood.

I worried myself into thinner clothes.
I prayed, walked with fear,
Jumped when I saw a retarded woman
Drool big gobs on her shoes,
Her eyes so loose they couldn't follow
A leaf seesawing from a tree.
At dinner I asked mother, who passed the butter
And said, It's Life. The nuns said prayers.
The priest made bell sounds and raised a chalice.
As far as I knew the earth didn't trouble
With me—earth smug with its toothy alps,
Five continents, a river so long
Egyptians could stand on the bank,
Hold hands, and never reach the sea.

This left me scared, and more scared
When at choir practice
—Catholics in green sweaters
Singing above the organ's squeeze
Of noise—I saw a girl from
My class drool on a high note,
Just a little, like a broken shoelace.
Disease, I thought, starts small
—string in the mouth—
And goes and goes until you're like that woman,
A noisy one with shadows in the head.

And now my classmate, two rows
To the left of me and years
Ahead in math. She's got it.
I made my eyes big, sang loud, sang
In the streets to keep the world from
Pushing into my third grade life with all its worry. ❧

When we fired our rifles
We spooked sparrows from the tree.
Bottles burst when we aimed,
Tin cans did more than *ping*
And throw themselves in dry grass.
The dog pulled in tail and ears,
Saddened his eyes and crawled under the car.
We smiled at this, Leonard and I,
And went to look at the tin cans
And push our fingers into the holes —
Pink worms wagging at our happiness.
We set them up again, blew jagged zeros
On all sides, and then sat down
To eat sandwiches, talk about girls,
School, and how to get by on five-dollar dates.
Finished eating, we called the dog
With finger snaps and tongue clicks,
But he crawled deeper into shadow.
We searched the car trunk for coke cans,
Found three, and set them further away.
We raised the rifles, winced an eye,
And fired, Leonard hitting
On the third try, me on the fifth.
We jumped up and down, laughed, and waved
A hand through the drifts of gun smoke,
Then the two of us returned to the car
Where we dragged the dog into the back seat.
We started the engine, let it idle in smoke,
And raised our rifles one last time,
The grass and dirt leaping into air.
We laughed and took a step back,
Packed the rifles in oily blankets,
And revved the engine. We turned onto the road
Without a good thought in our heads,
Ready for life. ❧

No one did much. Mornings, cats blinked
On steaming fences. Old neighbors
Raked what was already in piles,
Not looking up. The alley ran one way
Along our house where family looked out,
Broke as ever, with their watery eyes
Of piping soup. As I remember
Uncle was crazy; said he would end poverty
And its no nothing life by jogging,
By putting on muscle: rope inside
The arms, apples coming through on the stomach.
Boxing is the way to riches
He said. Mother drank tea and muttered
"Fool." Father teased the cat.
Grandfather in two sweaters played cards
By the window. I joined uncle
On my tricycle, that stool
Of squeaky parts, as I followed
Day after day. He never added a ring
Of flesh, my poor uncle jogging
In his funeral suit, in his miserable beard,
In his hair and its clicking lice.
No, he never carried the world
On his shoulders until he lay down in the grave,
Dead in the heart. And me?
I rode my tricycle, a tiny fire in my knees,
Two, almost three, apples on the stomach.
I wanted to live, bend bars with my teeth if I had to,
Lift whole towns if I must,
All for my life, my frolicking shoes,
And for uncle with a white flag in the chest,
A little salute to the stars. ❧

When I was five I found
Beauty—a girl on a box
Of soap—while fooling in
An alley with my brother
Who was all gum and
Better looks. He snatched
The box, gazed, and
Looked back at me, kid
With spiky hair and teeth
Like a broken-down fence
—said he knew her house
And took me down our alley
To the street Mother said never
To cross. "Over there,"
He pointed, "that house."
I worried my brow into lines:
Stacked boards, oily field
Of truck parts, a warehouse
Slamming shut with
Machinery. "No sir,"
I said, being no one's fool,
And ran away to play
Only to return, look both ways,
And cross the street.
I looked back. A river
Of glass and bottle
Caps gleamed on the asphalt.
The parked cars seemed far,
Even Rick who was jumping
In delight, singing I was a dead boy
On the floor when Momma found out.
"You're stupid too," I said,
Turned, and walked until
I was lost and talking
To a dog. And how did I
Get back? How did any of us
Get back when we searched

For beauty? I don't know,
Except days later
Our neighbor's cat crossed
That street and came home
With a sliver, long as an evil finger,
Poking from its eye.
Poor orange cat, it couldn't tear,
Blink, or close its eye in sleep,
Even in death. ❧

I can clear my name.
It was my brother, not me,
Who stole your fruit
And sold that pop
Bottle on your porch
(with our pennies we
Bought jaw breakers
That shattered like stars
When Mother got us home,
Naked with our two sins).
It was brother, not me.
I was saintly inside and out,
And walked through puddles
In a Catholic sweater,
Even though it was
Summer and no school.
Good on Sundays,
I could jump from a chair
And spell my name three times
Before I dropped to my feet.
I jumped from the fence,
The incinerator, the house
—air all around for
Seconds and me flapping
As I spelled the holy
Countries of the world,
Yugoslavia as best I could.
My brother watched,
Sister with a Tootsie Roll
That was yet another
Bottle from your porch
Watched with fangs
Of candy in her mouth.
They witnessed me hang
In the air. They shouted
For me to fly over the tree,
Your tree, and come back

With yellow-green apricots.
I leaped beyond the clothes
Line and found myself
In the bush, knocked with
Lumps where a halo would rest.
I touched this sparkling hurt
And ran inside to ask
Mother if there was blood.
Horns, she said
With her witch's mouth,
Devil horns! My sweater
Went limp on my body.
God gives me a mother
Like this? To hell
With the saints! I kicked
Puddles as I walked
To your house, not flew,
And let the apricots
And pop bottles alone.
While you watered
The front yard, I sneaked
Through the back door
And took a happy dollar
From your purse.
I laughed into my hands.
Horns, I whispered,
Big horns for me. 🙿

I want to stay in bed.
The heat is kicking the front door,
And our daughter, angel
In panties turned inside out,
Is chasing a fly with a toilet roll.

It's a game for her, anger for me,
That fly orbiting my head.
I pull the sheet over my face.
My wife is there,
Groaning that she doesn't want to get up.
She opens a red eye, and I close
Mine: I see the snow
Of give-away bank calendars,
Fruit, rocks hugged for their cold,
And clouds hauling in fall.

When I close my eyes
It's still there: the day
Sweating like a mule. What God
Invented summer? I need two washcloths,
A wet one to cool the body,
A dry one to hide my face
From what's coming:

The door opens.
A *clip-clop* enters the bedroom.
The mule. It hangs its head, big as a suitcase,
Over the bed. Flies whine from its ear,
Jump, make their sticky living off each toe. ❧

The new life is going to be a dirty blond,
A Sarah or Rebecca, and the house small
For children—two playing with a back yard dog,
One in the tree with the boyish sun.
You're home, father to a white family
That went wrong somewhere—stocks maybe,
A closed factory that's now shadow
A real daddy who fried eggs and then left for good.
Take over, Mr. Fill-In. The daughter, color
Of straw, is asking about the elephant,
And you say that he's as old as rocks,
Like these in the drive, or those over there.
Scratch them, you say, knock them good
With pliers. They won't break
But break sparks.

When you talk giraffes, stars,
Why red is red, the boys push away the dog
To sit at your side, almost touching,
And ask about fire and sky and valley.
Heat you say, blue you say, river fog you say
—answers that have them jumping in your lap,
Happy that their new daddy is a smart man,
Happy that Mama is smiling on the back steps
And touching your hair. You stand up,
And work creaks in your bones.
This is your wife with a playful finger
In your belt loop. These are children
At your legs and the dog leaping for a ball.
With coins jumbling in your pocket,
You walk them across the street to the store
—candy for the jaw, red juice for the tongue—
And talk of ice inside the world, blue and white
And square as a house. This is how it is.
The children walk in step, the wife hugs your waist,
And who's to say that you're not a man
Like no other and father to all. 🐾

God's away right now, but he'll be back,
A voice whispers. I slink into the bathtub.
Steam rises like incense off the water.
My penis is engorged. It's all right,
Another voice tells my left ear,
Go ahead and do it? I bite my lip,
Close my eyes because I'm too scared
To look, and listen instead to the small
Waves lick the edges of the bathtub
And spill over. When I stop, a voice says,
God saw you. The burning bush is going
To chase you. I drain the water,
Dry off, and think, There's too much
Steam for God to see.
                              The front yard.
It's still hot and, except for the crickets
In the flower bed, quiet. I start
Up the street. Where is everyone?
Before my bath there were kids
And parents and dogs licking pie tins.
Mom was watering and Rick was leaning on
The car fender looking cool. I flinch
When a sparrow shifts in the holly bush.
God, I'm in trouble. God made everyone disappear

Or so I believe until I see Mr. Grycz
On the front steps, and he's sweating a mouthful
Of hotdogs. Jutte his wife is just as greasy.
She flicks a finger of sweat at me
As I pass. She laughs, coughs,
And a noise like a wheelbarrow of rocks
Rattles in her chest. I ask,
Where is everyone? Jutte shrugs,
And says, They go to hell. They laugh
And rattle the rocks in their chests.

A piece of food falls from Mr. Grycz's mouth.
I pretend to like them. I laugh,
Take a step back. Laugh, take a step
Until I'm out of sight but thinking
That their marriage is old as trees.

Still, I want to get married when I learn to drive.
Andy, an older kid on the other street,
Said it feels like chicken,
And after he told me I went around not liking
Girls that much. I kept picturing
A hot, bald, salt-and-peppered chicken
Attached to my penis, and me in bed
And my brother in the bunk above me
Asking, What's going on? I tell him
I can't stop sweating. Of course
God is looking, and he whispers,
Then shouts loud enough for Mom to hear,
Leave the chicken alone, Gary.

Andy from the other street.
He should know. He's had his way
With the daughter of the peanut man,
A poor guy who works the mall:
One leg shorter, tiny American flags
In his hat and no one buying
Because we like sunflower seeds better.
Andy whom I helped carry cardboard
To a vacant lot. Here, he said,
Here, over here. We stomped the cardboard
Into a bed for his girl and set a brick
At each corner. My girl will love me
For the trouble, he said, and said,
This hole I dug is for Cokes,
And seeds, though she's bringing free peanuts.

But where is Andy now?
Where are my brother and sister,
And Mom? It's eerie when there's no one
Around to beat you up. Then a loud noise,
And I'm thinking that it's Mr. Grycz
Just breathing deeper, except I see
Mr. Wise's truck, and my Mom
In the cab, and the kids in the back,
Full of racket. Cross-eyed Johnny,
First to jump out, shouts at my shoulder
That a house on Belmont Ave. burned to the floor
And though no one died at least three cried,
And ain't that better than nothing?

God's going to have his way, in time, in time. ❧

The public library was saying things
In so many books,
And I, Catholic boy
In a green sweater,
Was reading the same page
A hundred times.
A girl was in my way,
Protestant or Jew,
And she was at the other end
Of the oak table,
Her hands like doves
On the encyclopedia, E–G.
England, I thought,
Germany before the war?
She'll copy from that book,
Cursive like waves
Riding to the shore,
And tomorrow walk across lawns
In a public school dress
With no guilt pulling at an ear.
And me? I'll kick
My Catholic shoes through
Leaves, stand in the
Cloakroom and eat
A friend's lunch. My work
Was never finished.
My maps were half-colored,
History a stab in the dark,
And fractions the inside
Of a pocket watch
Spilled on my desk.
I was no good. And who do I
Blame? That girl.

When she scribbled a pink
Eraser and her pony
Tails bounced like skirts,
I looked up, gazed for what
My mother and sister could not
Offer, then returned to
The same sentence: *the Nile*
Is the longest river in the world.
A pencil rolled from the
Table when she clicked open
Her binder. I looked up,
Gazed, looked back down:
The Nile is the longest river . . . ❧

We could be here. This is the valley
And its black strip of highway, big-eyed
With rabbits that won't get across.
Kids could make it, though.
They leap barefoot to the store—
Sweetness on their tongues, red stain of laughter.
A hot time falls from their palms,
Chinks of light, and they eat
Candies all the way home
Where there's a dog for each hand,
Cats, chickens in the yard.
A pot bangs and water runs in the kitchen.
Beans, they think, and beans it will be,
Brown soup that's muscle for fieldwork
And the tired steps to a fruit ladder.
Okie or Mexican, Jew that got lost,
It's a hard life where the sun looks.
The cotton gin stands tall in the money dream
And the mill is a paycheck for the wife,
Or perhaps even my wife, who once boxed peaches
And plums, hoed Papa's field that wavered like a mirage.
We could go back. I could lose my job,
This easy one that's only words,
And pick up a shovel, hoe, broom to take it
Away. Worry is my daughter's story.
She touches my hand. We suck roadside
Snowcones in the shade and look about.
Behind sunglasses I see where I stood: brown kid
Getting across. "He's like me,"
I tell my daughter, and she stops her mouth.
He looks both ways and then leaps
Across the road where riches
Happen on a red tongue. 🙦

The bulldozer ticks in the sun,
Yellow elephant that leaned against a house,
Groaned when the timbers groaned:
Two by fours, joists and beams,
Cornered joints, floor and paneled walls,
Yawning nails that have not held light in forty years.

What we threw down is raised up by others.
Ants march with feathery grains,
With timbers of twig, seed, torn blossoms,
The white of what they eat,
The black of what they bed down in.

Sparrows busy the wind with tracks,
And the worm links air and light,
And moss breathes in the throats of pipes,
And a blond silt gathers in piles in a dry pond,
And the fly sleeps on a shard of warm glass.

An orange cat creeps in blue shadows.
The diseased apricot is down, leans against the garage,
Its spooked limbs and branches parachuting white blossoms,
Still alive with the juice of the trunk,
Arc of sun and moon, chill that is spring.

Earlier a man in blue overalls himself crept,
Poked with shovels
Through debris, searched for memory,
The china plate, the bottle blue with age,
Scorched spoon and fork, buttons and jagged-toothed keys,
Coins with dead presidents — searched for tokens,
The value of metal with furred rust.

(He tossed a door into his battered truck,
Buckled paint cans and pipe. He started his engine,
Idled. When a tire dipped into a rain-pocked hole,
The windows rattled. Black smoke hung
In the air, and then was gone.)

Nature works a poor block.
The once silent frog fills with air.
The gopher and robin stir,
The mice with their candles of yellow teeth.
The grass, once cornered by cement,
Now itches for life and feeds on the tiniest cracks. &

America is at work. There is the splotch of blue neon
Behind the left leg, renegade line in the right eye.
My favorite waitress is walking three hot plates,

The enchilada special with extra red
And a row of olives crucified by toothpicks.
She bounces from table to table,

With the lead-stink of bitterness on her tongue,
With the vinegary rag to wipe up what the Fat Boys
Let fall from their drunken forks.

The cluttered table is where the mad ate.
Their mess is her mess; her breasts shake
Their sweaty holsters as she digs fingernails

Into dried egg and scrubs. Her skirt goes up
Like a curtain when she bends for a clean spoon.
No one bothers to turn. The patrons

Stir their coffee, poke the yellow
From snotty eggs, and eat with faces close
To their plates. America is at work.

Look at Grandpa go to town on fried chicken,
The ketchup coughing from the bottle. The appliance
Salesman in the plaid coat knows. His sucked thumb

Is just another meat, the music a fly-noise
In a cracked speaker, and the mop the Negro handles
The slosh in the belly. Appliance guy pulls

At his pants, pays, and pays again when he turns
To the glazed donuts sweating behind glass.
A moist hand grabs one, no two,

For the sweet drive three blocks home. ❧

Stray dogs come with the rain,
Two hours before the garbage men
And their elephant noise of truck
Crushing eggshell and tuna can,
Light bulbs with their bleak rattle.
Or so I hear. I struggle into slippers,
Part the curtain: a tall dog,
Paws up on the heap, is
Working on a sour casserole,
The noodles marching into his mouth,
And a moist nose sniffing
For chicken bone and week-old stew,
For pie tins with buttery crust.
I've never seen happiness
Over a bone with little meat,
Happiness in rain. This
Is what I want, to be up before light,
To be in rain with garbage men
On the back porch, I snap
A finger, call, "Here boy,"
And the dog throws down its ears,
Ashamed to be caught eating.
I show him the pink emptiness of my palm,
But what am I to him? He doesn't know me.
I'm a man in a robe, not a friend
Of green alleys and poor days,
A man in slippers clomping
Pathetically down wet stairs.
Hurried love trots away on three legs,
The hurt paw touching ground
Only when he looks back. ❧

No one swims better than me.
I like the water blue and mountainous along the edges,
My arms tucked to my side, my crocodile head
Floating on the surface with a mad beard of bubbles.

The apples of youth show up in arms,
On the notched stomachs of kids sunning on towels,
In faces, in the calves of young girls
Stepping into the pool. When I step in,
Water spills over the edges and the bee drinks.
When I dog-paddle, brave kids ride my back like leeches.
When I stand on the diving board,
Gravity tips toward the water.
Swimmers in seahorse trunks stare
And mothers cower from the broken mirror of water.

But what can I do? Swim three strokes
And climb out to sit in the shade with a thermos of Kool-Aid
And my one long sandwich with its plywood of meats.
I turn on my transistor, butter myself with sunscreen,
Wiggle flies from my toes.
                    I love God
Because he thought of water,
I love man because he invented Saturdays.
I admire the lifeguards with their chrome whistles,
Their noses tipped white, the ladders of hair
That climb their legs. I love the kids
Who love me. They come over like ducks
And watch me squeeze the flesh of my knees
To make faces. Here's one of Elvis,
Here's one of Princess Di, our stone presidents of
Mt. Rushmore. I give them Tootsie Rolls
And watch them chew the juicy mud of candy.

They only beg twice to get me to jump
From the sides—the water, shaped into a hand,
Slaps the red bathers in lounge chairs.
During the week I make ball bearings. Life turns
That way, and I get to eat. I sweat
In coveralls, in boots, in a striped engineer's cap.
The air of factory work is a flame inside
The lungs, this scar a pink reminder.
On Saturdays I wear a flowery shirt, sunglasses
And Panama hat, towel over my shoulder,
Thongs on my fleshy feet.
I take my time when I dress at home,
And do the same in public, one happy button
At a time and a whistle on my lips.
When I swim, friend, I have nothing to hide. ❧

SATURDAY WALK

IN CROCKETT, CALIFORNIA

In this town the weeds grow wilder than kids,
Then flatten in fall. It's fall now,
And a friend and I, bored with the holes
In our souls are walking up and down
The streets looking for breaks, scars,
A jackhammer splitting black crumbs of asphalt.
No one rips a yellow bedsheet in two,
No one peels the bacon strip of Band-Aid;
No one coughs or bothers about the holes
In the street. They care even less
About us, or the blue-eyed dogs that follow,
Then fall off. The cartwheeling paper bag
Holds more interest. We feel the same,
And climb a hill to admire the C & H sugar plant,
Black with the shadow of workers.
White smoke unravels from a stack.
Metal clicks. Yellow forklifts,
Those dinosaurs that run on gas
And a good kick, are coming alive.
This town does make noise after all.
We climb down on the heels of our dusty shoes
And at the entrance to the factory
A guard stops us. We ask about tours,
But he points to the museum across the street.
We go there to stare at photographs
Behind glass, quilts on the walls,
Piles of sugar on scales, bathing beauties
Of fly-flecked calendars. We pay homage to
Six blow-ups of the town's favorite son: Aldo Rey.
We handle horseshoes and ball bearings,
Grip the spokes of monstrous wagon wheels,
Study blue teacups, more photographs,
More piles of sugar—relics hauled
From abandoned houses. When we leave
The museum guide rattles a packet of sugar at us.
We thank him and he thanks us,

And the three of us stand for a moment
Smiling a lot of different ways.
We leave, then, and walk up one street.
No kids in the front yard,
No men in the back yard under arbors.
It's quiet. The leaves, buckled red by fall,
Make more noise. We return to the car
To sit on the fenders.
We like this town. It doesn't talk too much.
Their radios tremble low behind curtains
And old men empty the benches at noon.
Nothing is for show. The lawns are shaggy,
The trees are haywire.
Worry is no more than flattened grass,
Maybe one less paycheck when the Teamsters
Go on strike, maybe a bad transmission
In a good car. The people work hard,
Sweat. In turn, the plant does its best
To sweeten the air. 🙠

THREE ❧

I can stay what I am, a little crazy in jeans,
And drive across town to look for a fight.

It's Saturday. At the studio we spar on this day,
Roundhouse and spinback, reverse punch

And ax kick that's a broken branch on a shoulder.
Ten minutes with black James and Filipino Bobby,

Dennis the white gardener. We rest against the wall,
Wet as snails. Wind is what we want, a little rest.

But we rise to our feet, stretch, and throw
Kicks at the air, and bowing to one another,

Begin to make bruises where the heart won't go,
A hurt won't stay. I like that, the thrust of bone,

And how if I'm hit I'll step in, almost crazed,
And sweep, back fist, and maybe take him down.

Later, I dress, cup and shin guards under my jeans
And with a nappy head friend walk the city.

America needs a beating. We look for those people,
Happily do our part, and race around buildings,

He to black Oakland and I to the white side of
Berkeley. My hands hurt in the shower. My face stings

Over dinner where we talk movies, books, and test
Our spelling—Eurydice, rhomboid, cornucopia—

Because the mind must be as right as the body.
My wife thinks I'm crazy. Still, she clears the

Table and stays. Still she joins us in the living
Room with magazines and chess. Mariko and I play

First. She makes a move, and while she waits for me
Spells new words and lifts a dumbbell,

A coke can, twenty reps to an arm. My wife thinks
Nothing of this; it goes on every night.

I make my move and ask Mariko, Who's Atlas?
She doesn't look up when she takes a rook from me—

The man who holds up the world. I ask about
Perseus and the river Styx, and she knows in her way,

I stand up, What is this? I throw a sidekick
And she says, Sidekick . . . but this is better.

She throws a roundhouse, so perfect that her mother
Puts down her magazine. We smile at our little one,

This child of the 80s. Rising, my wife throws a kick,
I throw another, and Mariko does a turnback,

Waits, and flicks a knifehand block to my hip
—all three of us bounce from foot to foot,

Spelling words, laughing, readying for the world. ❧

The perfect life overturns like a red wagon.
My wife is doing her nails.
Her breasts are heavy, she is late,
And I'm pacing up and down like a mad doctor.

Now I see it all:
A baby fat as a waterbottle
Swaddled in a blue blanket.
Is he smiling for Grandma's Kodak?
Is he burping the milk of pleasure?
Is he kicking his feet for song?
No, he's grunting with one hand on my nose.

Adios to my Italian clothes,
My rack of wines, my dear friends,
My car glinting evilness on all four bumpers,
The crown of cleverness on my head deflating like a cake.

Adios to my weekend trips,
Pacific Grove where, behind the finely ground lenses
Of German binoculars, the sea is blue as a made-up heaven;
Where whales sing, tourists look,
And the three-flavored ice cream cones totter
In our hands
As we go from shop to shop.

The good life ends.
Evenings I will stay home
And watch the fireplace with its saw of red flames,
My daughter reading, my wife reading,
My pitbull Apollo cleaning a paw,
With Dinner Jazz on the radio,
Piano noise like the footsteps of a divorced man
Walking up stairs. I will stare
At my bank book, worry my brow into lines,
And rinse my throwaway shaver over and over.

Now what will my daughter say?
Cry? Lecture me on self-control?
Conspire with Apollo, heathen dog
Who, I know in my heart, has always eyed
My legs as a second helping of Mexican food.

I'm too old to start over. The hair
On my pillow could smother a kingly rat.
My brow is lined, my bones a wobbly chair.
Give a week, a month, he'll be here,
Bundle that's my life, child for the next century,
Hoodlum out for my sleep, my son, my son,
Bald, pink, with fists beating sparks from my sleeping eyes. ❧

Piaf, just what are you saying?
Three songs, sherry not yet dry
On the tongue, newspapers twisted
Into busy wreaths of fire,
And I turn to my daughter,
Little thinker on the couch.
She looks away. She doesn't want
Anything to do with failure,
These songs that don't make sense
At any speed. I go alone,
Guessing what it all means
—*poulet* is "pole" and *poulet*
Au vinaigre is "my pole
Has many vines." I listen
At the window. The flute has told
Me more, the violin, the drum
That banged like the guillotine.
Still, I don't know enough.
I play them again.
                                    I close
My eyes, rest. Is it Seurat
And his river banks, or maybe
Van Gogh in yellow rooms, the
Stuff of postcards? Is it rain,
Rain and bricked streets that lead to
Adultery on a squeaky bed,
The stuff of movies? Piaf's voice
Is the giveaway, scrawny
Bird huddled on a lone wire,
Flogged by wind and bad romance.

I think I know. The sherry
Brings on the clouds, fogged-up
Lenses above my neighbor's trees,
And here, at the front window,
Sorrow is a lawnful of
Birds who, like us, share the green,
Make noises in pairs, and then,
Without so much as a word,
Go alone in the air. 🕊

SETTLING MATTERS AT A YUGOSLAVIAN BAR

for George Evans

Let me try again. You were in love
With the dental hygienist, not me.
I was crying inside for the florist,
Big woman with little moons of earth
Under her fingernails. You did most
Of the talking, hinted that we were famous
Architects, owned cars and California houses,
And spread monogrammed beach blankets
On the Mexican Riviera, in December.
Our *real* riviera, you now admit,
Is a sour river outside Fresno,
Three tiny fish trying to climb out
Because chemicals hurt. You talked,
Not me. I laughed only when
You kicked my leg. I drank my beer,
Made a hundred famous faces
By moving my eyebrows one at a time,
And scissored my cigarette
Between fingers, very European.
Again, you talked, not me. You said,
The Seine rushes through my heart,
And kicked my leg. You said,
The bud of life is with you,
And kicked my leg. The women drank
Their drinks through vein-colored straws,
Drank and played with their plastic umbrellas.
They said, We like all kinds
Of music. California is nice.
O San Francisco, a pretty place.
You peeled the label off your beer
Bottle and I made more interesting faces.
We both stopped when they said,
Excuse us, and wobbled to the restroom.

We huddled our faces together.
You asked, How we doing? and I asked,
Can we afford more umbrella drinks?
They returned with their coats buttoned
To their throats, said, O San Francisco,
A pretty place but we have to go,
And waved goodbye with their fingers.
We kicked each other's legs
So we could laugh, waved stiffly
And lowered our faces into our beers,
The flatness of life. We ran
Our hands through our hair, paid,
Then left twirling the plastic umbrellas,
Gifts for our wives who were just then
Slipping into the shower on California time. ❧

The French movie star takes off her blouse,
Puts it back on. Nothing
For you Pierre,
This week,
Next week,
And if I have it my way,
As long as that thing stands up.

The movie ends.
The patrons blink when the lights come on.
I help my wife with her coat;
My friend helps his wife with her coat.
The men around us are just as helpful.
Are any of them like me,
Confused about what they just saw,
Two hours of bedroom crying?
And why did the old nun beat herself with a candle?
What was this about a saint with a flying cape?
Where did the mouse come from
When the violins started?
(Poor, brie-fed mouse, ten minutes
On camera and no credit in the end.)

Outside, the stars mingle with neon.
The faces of newspapers drink from the gutter.
We walk back to the car, the four
Of us smiling. What was it
About? I look back: the marquee glows "psycho-drama."
That's what I need in life. Lust is a slow slime
In the heart. I nudge against my friend's
Wife's tear-shaped ass. She's beautiful.
I've seen her hang laundry and board a bus
In high heels. "Psycho-drama," I breathe
In her ear. She squeals, laughs, and tells
Her husband, "Honey, he's doing it again!"

Honey punches me in the arm,
Softly. "Psycho-drama," he says,
And places a creepy kiss on my screaming wife's mouth. &

My daughter runs outside to busy
Herself with tiny cakes of mud.
"It's important," she says,
Not wanting to hear my poor stories again.
Still I drag her to the car
And the short climb to the Berkeley
Hills, for gardens are in bloom,
Red thing and yellow this and that.
Trees with rootfuls of clouds
Line the walk. "They're older than me,"
I say, and she won't look at them
Or the grandma houses,
Quaint as tea cups.

The rich seem never to come out
Of their houses. They never sit on
Lawns, or bang a ball against
The garage door, or water the green strip
Along the street—hose in one hand.
Can of beer in the other.
At our place, the flowers fall
When we turn a hose on them
—even the pepper tree, rigged
With wire and rope, fell over
Like the neck of a sick giraffe.

I talk and talk. I say the poor
Rave about the color orange
And the rich yammer over egg-white.
I put this to Mariko, steps ahead,
A plucked branch dragging in her hand,
And begin again, a bore to the end.
When I was like you, I picked
Grapes like nobody's business...

She starts to skip. I walk faster,
Loud as a fool. When I was a kid,
I lugged oranges and shared plums with Okies...
But she's on the run, the branch
Fluttering like a green fire
Because the corner is up ahead
And an evening without me
Can't be far beyond. 🙐

Television is a slashed fish
Of color. We eat sandwiches, drink milk,
And love the story of a man losing
His wife to another, the car crash,
The foul language that lingers
Like gas. The program ends,
And the slashed fish drains from
Our faces. We climb from bed,
Shower, and climb back into bed.
We open books, and it's the same story,
Men losing women, women losing men
To other men, and people losing
Themselves altogether — the dead
On their wheelless carts
Stalled on the way to a snowy heaven.
We can't get enough. The hero
Overturns his car and three sparks
Burn the town. The heroine
Lets down her hair and says, I hurt.
Reckless birds skim the icy pages
Of river where these lovers walk,
Almost touching, almost untying
Words from o-shaped mouths.
Fish jump from the river onto our cheeks,
Pink of salmon, oxygen, slippery
Flop on the bank. The good part
Has come, the *yes yes yes,*
And for us who are more than words,
Less than hero or heroine,
The lights go out. 🙐

Ok, you're wealthy, and dinner is served in courses,
And with each course a man, hired for the occasion,
Stands up on your palate and applauds,
Then sits back down. A good time
Should last only so long. The ride
In a rented yacht should last until lunch,
And a movie-made-for-TV, a 300-page novel,
A tennis game in whites. Push-ups affect your arms,
Dry as they are, and jumping rope
Can ruin a favorite sweater. You're getting ready
For tomorrow. Tomorrow comes with applause.
At a rich friend's ranch, you pull yourself onto a horse
And the horse creaks leather and clops his hooves,
Sweats and bangs his cock on one flank then the other.
You sweat too because you're racing shadows.
Dark circles show up under your arms.
When you dismount, the soul applauds.
Your wife applauds, the lackey unhooking the saddle applauds.
A day was never so pleasant. The clouds are tidy,
Like a row of white socks, and the sky, as you say, beams.
You drink iced tea in a wicker chair. Your smile
Can go only so far when everyone laughs.
Your mind wanders. You have not had enough,
You tell everyone, and they applaud with their fingertips
As you walk away. At the red barn, you choose
A scythe and begin to whack brush on a hillside.
The sweat starts again, slime under each arm.
You know a good time should last until dusk
But you can't help yourself. You whack the weeds
And pat the dusty horse who has come over to look.
But friend, if the horse were smarter,
He would laugh at you, not applaud. He sweats
For his hay, and that's the best he can do.
You can do better, but you like sweating
Because it brings on smells. Now look at you.

When the horse begins to pee, you think, It's applauding,
It's beautiful. You do the same. The man inside
Wipes his face and strains a small stream
Onto the ground. The horse stares and stares,
Then lets loose again. The liquid a horse can splash
Lures a wealthy man with a scythe in his hand. 🙠

Long-legged mosquitoes feed on algae and transient blood,
Pond water with its sullen frogs. Elephants feed on straw
And lions red meat on a caretaker's sharp stick.
Rats, those black sleds of evil,
Desire carrots, and camels oats,
And wolves smashed meat the color of perfect lungs.
It's a Sunday for you, hot with sun
And breeze-dead eucalyptus. As you push a stroller,
Your wife leaves red smears on her cigarettes
And your child laps cotton candy—
Flies have a hard time peeling off.
You shoo them away, scold the monkeys
Who scold you. You throw peanuts
And all of monkey island jump up and down,
Not unlike children when lollipops are yanked
From their mouths. The giraffes are feeding on leaves,
Goats brick-colored pellets, and water buffaloes leafy soup
In a trough. You make a face,
But smile at a watchful mother nursing her fawn.
The lynx, black bear, polar bear, sloth
All wake when the locks turn. They'll eat now,
And the foreign birds will eat when they please.
They flitter in wet shadows; they dip hooked beaks
Into tuna cans and come up with seed.
Your wife crushes another cigarette,
Your son drops his cotton candy. An hour in the zoo
Makes you hungry. You buy pink popcorn, leave,
And sit on grass near a pond
Where dirty boys are dragging nets for catfish.
The popcorn is loud in ear and jaw when you chew.
You faintly hear the boys scream "Got one
I got one." Catfish will pant for the kind of air
They like, and finding none,
Flop and die with one eye in the hundred-degree sun. ❧

It's not the night's fault.
The violins have tried to make the shirts,
Still hung on the wires, get up and find bodies.
It's no one's fault that the chic are gone.
A man with no legs is propped up in a doorway —
Teddy bear legs, cut off at the knees.
I shake a sweaty coin in his hands.
Later his nephew will come to take him home,
Maybe carry him under his arm like a box,
Maybe let him stand on his shoulders,
A circus act taken to the streets.

In the windows the mannequins are stiff as ever —
If you were to knock on them with a knuckle,
Dust would cry from their eyes,
They're bored of standing bent just so.
I'm like a mannequin. The dust of boredom
Weeps from my eyes, sprays from my nostrils,
Jumps from my hair. I'm dust inside, dust
Of boredom and cars that breathed on me for years.

I have nothing to pass on, to tell a son.
It's easy to poke a hole in snow,
Easy to drive a car with two hands, drink
With your mouth, sleep with your eyes closed.
But how does this knowledge help?
It won't earn a diploma, certainly not make money,
And money is what he'll need to support my dreams,
Women with their breasts like a handful of sand.

A horse of smells. I look back.
It's the man with no legs. He's pushing himself
Toward me on a rickety platform of skates.
I hurry away, only to stumble
Into his blind cousin, sores the color of bacon.
I offer coins, and one to a grandma in shawl,
Two to a boy with a face of black smoke.

I enter a bar called Over the Skies of Acapulco.
The talk there is like digestion,
Quiet then suddenly loud.
After one drink I leave
Because the man on the squeaky stool next to me
Is speaking about his wife, no his lover,
His wife's first lover.

Why any of this?
The poor who envy the rich,
And the rich who despise the lonely,
The lonely in love with cereal that floats.

I'm getting the hell out.
I'm going to take these hands that work best
While I'm asleep. And some clothes.
The forest is green and made up of air. ❧

Ars Poetica, or Mazatlan, on a Day When Bodies Wash to the Shore

The body's in the morgue,
And the morgue's on this street
Where we're standing, Omar and I,
Invisible to the taxis and the mules
And the sleeping dogs
In the train station's shadow.

Earlier, we were at the mercado,
With its upside-down chickens
Blinking blood from all holes.
(We bought lemons and made bitter faces at oranges.)
Earlier, we were throwing down coins
In restaurants, big shots from
The North, because our hearts were full
And our wallets sandwiches for the dancing poor.

Now we're not so sure.
It's death that rode in with the waves
While we stood ankle-deep,
Backs toward the shore, the sky slashed
White where the blue would not go.
Death is the body of a man
With his arms forced into bent Ls,
With his hair whipping his eyes for not seeing,
With his belly, half of the world the ant can't climb.

Now we're not so sure.
The heat shimmers the leaves on the trees.
The taxis are asleep at jammed meters
And the children, once busy with balls,
Are eating the caked ice cream along their arms.
The truth is, we want to go home,
Vanish in the train's white smoke,
And miraculously find ourselves

In America. Omar, I ask, have you had enough?
He raises his face to mine,
Taps a cigarette against a yellow thumb
And strikes a blue flame.

No, we can't go. Our business
Is unfinished. I know this; Omar knows this.
We'll clomp down like mules to the shore,
Test the water with a hoof, and walk in
Until our heads lie on water, are covered by water.
If we come up, our teeth will flash signals
To those who've gathered—
Stout man, two old mothers, kids and their bikes
We live! We live! Crabs, with snapping claws,
Race to where they think we may wash
To the shore, legs first. 🐚

Books by Gary Soto

This book was typeset by
On Line Typography,
San Francisco

Cover and book design by
Nancy Brescia

Cover illustration by
Scott Sawyer